Year of

October 2012-November 2013

Edited by
Barry R. Pearlman

All booklets are published thanks to the
generous support of the members of the
Catholic Truth Society

CATHOLIC TRUTH SOCIETY
PUBLISHERS TO THE HOLY SEE

Contents

ISBN: 978 1 86082 818 8

A Gift of Faith

It is all that is good, everything that is perfect, which is given us from above; it comes down from the Father of all light; with him there is no such thing as alteration, no shadow of a change.[1]

God's grace is at the very beginning of faith in Christ: "because it is by grace that you have been saved, through faith; not by anything of your own, but by a gift from God; not by anything you have done, so that nobody can claim the credit."[2] This grace is freely created by God, and informs our faculties, effecting faith within our souls. It endows our intellects with understanding and intuition, by various means - such as the spoken word, the majesty of creation, the heroic virtue of the saints, or the intimations of the heart - which inspire the soul to believe in Christ. "We can contemplate God not only outside us and within us but also above us: outside through his vestiges, within through his image, and above through the light which shines upon our minds, which is the light of Eternal Truth, since our mind itself is formed immediately by Truth itself."[3]

This grace also affects our wills through the Spirit of love which makes Christ Jesus desirable and worshipful to the believer. Raised above natural reason, we come to trust in the Person of Jesus. Because it is of divine origin, faith secures the believer in a sure conviction, simply because *it places its trust in the One revealing*. We are then able to confess that Jesus is the Christ, the Son of the living God: not by our own "flesh and blood," but by the grace of our heavenly Father who revealed it.[4]

The author of Hebrews refers to this gift of faith as "knowledge of the truth" and proving "the existence of the realities that at present remain unseen."[5] Faith is a supernatural virtue, freely given, which disposes the whole person *firmly to assent to those truths revealed by God*, in the Holy Scriptures and the teachings of Holy Church, because he is truth itself.[6]

Without revelation our reasoning is aimless. Our limited minds merely receive information via the senses, while reason by its own light simply deduces and judges. So reason is powerless to create truth, especially the Uncreated Truth of God. Even though reason and evidence can prepare for faith by making belief convincing (or by inferring the divine ideas each thing reflects), only God can give that illumination which awakens trust in him, converting natural, reasoned belief into supernatural, trusting faith: *credo ut intelligere* (I believe in order to understand).

The faith we are proclaiming is our faith in Jesus Christ. Merely to believe in the existence of God is not yet faith. Such belief is but a natural conviction of the light of reason supported by evidence from creation: "For what can be known about God is perfectly plain to them since God himself has made it plain. Ever since God created the world his everlasting power and deity - however invisible - have been there for the mind to see in the things he has made."[7] But faith in Christ, being from above, is different in kind. It is a supernatural gift which imparts certainty - not the certainty of reason and evidence - but an interior conviction born of a personal experience of Christ.

It is through the indwelling of the Holy Spirit in us by faith that God the Father and the Son are made present, enabling us to participate in the life of the Holy Trinity. The soul thus informed and invigorated is capable of living a life more holy and spiritual than those who remain in the natural state. Increasing in virtue, the soul becomes more beautiful and more pleasing to the Father, because it is coming to resemble the Son in virtue and in truth. Insofar as the individual conforms to the likeness of God through the graces infused into the soul, so one becomes transformed to what God loves to the uttermost: his Son.

God's love for us is such that he wills we become the unvarnished image of the Son, because God, who always acts in accordance with his own wisdom, does everything for the glory of his Son who *is* the Wisdom of the Father.[8] And just as the Logos lovingly submits to the will of the Father in being the splendour of the Father, so analogously we, in our faithful submission to the will of Christ, mirror him as our love for God and for others radiates. Suffused ever more fully with the life of Christ, which is his Spirit living within us, we become a "light for the world" drawing others to Christ, thereby fulfilling our vocations as faithful followers of Our Lord.

Now holiness requires certain actions in obedience to Christ such as: prayer, worship, the Mass, charity, works of mercy, penance, study of the Scriptures, self-discipline, etc. These sow the words of Jesus into our relationships with others spreading the kingdom as does the mustard seed which becomes a great tree. These are the works that faith happily accomplishes. Without such works faith is dead.[9] It is precisely through such patient, and oftentimes courageous, perseverance that faith purges us of all that would separate us from the knowledge and fullness of God. This constancy in obedience lends faith this purgative capacity because it is faith that inspires the devout to say "Thy will, not my will." Authentic, humble faith predisposes one to obey God's word: *fiat mihi secundum verbum tuum.* Therefore, "it is impossible to please God without faith."[10]

But much more than this, faith makes us participants (*consortes divinae naturae*) in the divine life and thought. By faith, God's wisdom becomes our wisdom, his knowledge our knowledge, and his Spirit our spirit. For as the Father begets the Son for the sake of the love he has for the Son - who in turn comes from the Father glorifying and honouring him as his image - so we, in receiving through faith the graces which render us more pleasing to the Father, then love the Father *with the very Spirit of Christ in us*, and glorify the Father with the glory of the life of Christ within us. "I have given them the glory you gave to me, that they may be one as we are one. With me in them and you in me, may they be so completely one that the world will realise that it was you who sent me and that I have loved them as much as you loved me."[11]

In the fruitfulness of the Spirit, the Father generates the Son, and in the Spirit of submission the Son glorifies his Father. Thus, as the Holy Spirit is the substance of both this fertile, generating love (from the Father) and this resplendent, glorifying love (from the Son), so we also return this love to the Father through the self-giving of his Son in us. Then all we accomplish or endure becomes a sweet oblation to God. And our lives become a perpetual prayer - our crosses a triumph - and all of existence betrays a hidden grace.[12]

Such sanctity would be beyond us were it not for Christ's gift of the Church and her sacraments. The holy Catholic Church safeguards us in the truth, handed down to us from the Apostles. Her liturgy and traditions form and strengthen our faith. And her sacraments infuse grace into our hearts.

In other words, brothers, through the blood of Jesus we have the right to enter the sanctuary, by a new way which he has opened for us, a living opening through the curtain, that is to say, his body. And we have the supreme high priest over all the house of God. So as we go in, let us be sincere in heart and filled with faith, our minds sprinkled and free from any trace of bad conscience and our bodies washed with pure water. Let us keep firm in the hope we profess, because the one who made the promise is faithful.[13]

Thus, we are "certain of this: neither death nor life, no angel, no prince, nothing that exists, nothing still to come, not any power, or height or depth, nor any created thing, can ever come between us and the love of God made visible in Christ Jesus our Lord."[14]

* * *

Since faith is our response to the very life of Christ in us quickened by his Holy Spirit and nourished by the sacraments of the Church, it follows that our faith necessarily receives its vitality through prayer. Therefore, the prayers contained in this volume are compiled to nurture this gift of faith by focussing on various themes which imply the truths of Catholic teaching, as found in the creeds, the Catechism of the Church, her liturgy, devotion to Our Lady, and the traditions of the saints. In particular, this book is compiled according to the intentions of the

Holy Father, Pope Benedict XVI, for the Year of Faith as given in his document *Porta Fidei* (door of faith).[15] The pastoral recommendations given by the Congregation for the Doctrine of Faith states that this "Year" is "intended to contribute to a renewed conversion to the Lord Jesus and to the rediscovery of faith." To this end the prayers, novenas, and meditations contained herein reflect and present the richness of the Catholic faith from the earliest sources to more modern forms, in varying lengths and degrees of profundity, all selected to inform, strengthen, deepen, and enrich your life in Christ.

> Out of his infinite glory, may he give you the power through his Spirit for your hidden self to grow strong, so that Christ may live in your hearts through faith, and then, planted in love and built on love, you will with all the saints have strength to grasp the breadth and the length, the height and the depth; until, knowing the love of Christ, which is beyond all knowledge, you are filled with the utter fullness of God.[16]

The Holy Father's Prayer for the Year of Faith

Spirit of Life,
which in the beginning hovered over the abyss,
Help humanity of our time to understand
that the exclusion of God
leads to being lost in the desert of the world.
And that only where faith enters,
do dignity and liberty flourish
and the whole society is built on justice.
Spirit of Pentecost,
which makes of the Church one Body,
restore in the baptised
an authentic experience of communion;
render yourself a living sign
of the presence of the Risen One in the world,
a community of saints that lives in the service of charity.
Holy Spirit, which trains to the mission,
make us recognise that, also in our time,
so many persons are in search of the truth
about their existence and the world.
Make us collaborators of their joy with
the proclamation of the Gospel of Jesus Christ,
grain of the wheat of God, which renders good the terrain
of life and assures the abundance of the harvest.
Amen.

Prayers to the Most Holy Trinity

Meditation

With firm faith I believe and lovingly confess with joy that although thou, God, art most simple and one, having one only divinity and essence, nevertheless, thou art three Persons in one God, Father, Son and Holy Spirit. For thou art eternal, immense and perfect. Thou art of most wise intelligence…Thou, therefore, dost know, understand and contemplate thyself eternally always, actually, perfectly, comprehensively…Thou dost express, utter, conceive and produce within thyself that which thou knowest and understandest concerning thyself. And this utterance spoken within thyself…is thy Word coeternal, unchangeable and equal in all things to thee.

Moreover, I believe and confess with love and joy that thou Father…dost also eternally and perfectly love him as thyself, with an essential love which is neither personally nor really distinguished from thyself and thy Son. And thou, O Son…dost likewise eternally and perfectly love him with that same essential love. And from this mutual complacency of yours, O Father and Son, you breathe forth and produce from all eternity that love which is the sweetest embrace of both your indissoluble bond. This love is called the Holy Spirit, personally distinct from the Father and the Son...one with you, true eternal and illimitable God.

J. Michael de Coutances
Forty-fifth general of the Carthusian Order, 1597

Hymn

Come ye people,
   let us adore God in three persons:
The Father in the Son,
   with the Holy Spirit,
For the Father from everlasting
   begets the Word,
   who shares his Kingdom
   and his eternity,
And the Holy Spirit is in the Father,
glorified with the Son,
   a single power,
   a single essence,
   a single Godhead.
This it is whom we adore, saying:
Holy God, who didst create all by thy Son
   with the aid of the Holy Spirit;
Holy and Strong,
   by whom we have come to know the Father,
   by whom the Holy Spirit
   has come into the world;

Holy and Immortal,
Spirit of Consolation,
  who dost proceed from the Father
  and dwellest in the Son:
glory be to thee, O Holy Trinity!

Great Vespers of Pentecost in the Byzantine Rite

Prayer

You are holy, Lord, the only God,
  and your deeds are wonderful.
You are strong.
You are great.
You are the Most High,
you are almighty.
You, Holy Father, are King of heaven and earth.

You are Three and One,
Lord God, all good.
You are good, all good, supreme good,
Lord God, living and true.
You are love,
you are wisdom,
you are humility,
you are endurance.
You are rest,
you are peace.

You are joy and gladness.
You are justice and moderation.
You are all our riches,
and you suffice for us.

You are beauty.
You are gentleness.
You are our protector,
you are our guardian and defender.
You are courage.
You are our haven and our hope.
You are our faith,
our great consolation.
You are our eternal life,
great and wonderful Lord,
God almighty,
merciful Saviour.

St Francis of Assisi
Praises of God

For Faith in the Father

Meditation

This is the measure of the holiness of the children of God: "to be holy as God, to be holy with the holiness of God" [*Jn* 3:3]; and we do this by living close to Him in the depths of the bottomless abyss within. Then the soul seems in some way to resemble God who, even though He delights in all things, yet does not delight in them as much as he does in Himself, for He possesses within Himself a super-eminent good before which all others disappear. Thus all the joys which the soul receives are so many reminders inviting her to enjoy by preference the good she already possesses and to which nothing else can compare. "Our Father who art in Heaven…." It is in this little heaven that He had made in the centre of our soul that we must seek Him and above all where we must remain.

St Elizabeth of the Trinity
Heaven in Faith

Psalm

The Lord is my shepherd;
there is nothing I shall want.
Fresh and green are the pastures
where he gives me repose.

Near restful waters he leads me,
to revive my drooping spirit.

He guides me along the right path;
he is true to his name.
If I should walk in the valley of darkness
no evil would I fear.
You are there with your crook and your staff;
with these you give me comfort.

You have prepared a banquet for me
in the sight of my foes.
My head you have anointed with oil;
my cup is overflowing.

Surely goodness and kindness shall follow me
all the days of my life.
In the Lord's own house shall I dwell
for ever and ever.

Psalm 22 (23)

Prayer

O Lord my God,
teach my heart where and how to seek you,
   where and how to find you.
Lord, you are my God and my Lord,
   and never have I seen you.

You have created me and re-created me
and you have given me all the good things I possess,
   and still I do not know you.
I have not yet accomplished that for which I was made.

Poor, I have come to one who is rich.
Unfortunate, I have come to one who is merciful.
Do not let me return scorned and empty-handed.
Let me discern your light whether from afar
    or from the depths.

Teach me to seek you and reveal yourself to me as I seek,
for I can neither seek you if you do not teach me how,
nor find you unless you reveal yourself.

Let me seek you in desiring you;
let me desire you in seeking you;
let me find you in loving you;
    let me love you in finding you.

I acknowledge, Lord, and give thanks
    that you have created your image in me,
so that I may recollect you,
think of you,
love you.

For I do not seek to understand so that I may believe;
but I believe so that I may understand.
For I believe this also, that "unless I believe,
I shall not understand" [*Is* 7:9].
Lord, grant that I may understand
as you see fit.

Saint Anselm,
From the *Proslogion*

For Faith in the Son

Meditation

It is true that the end of all desires is happiness, which is a
perfect state with the presence of all goods. No one reaches
this state except by an ultimate union with him who is the
fountain and origin of all goods that are both natural and
gratuitous, both bodily and spiritual, both temporal and
eternal. And this is the one who said of himself: "*I am the
Alpha and the Omega, the beginning and the end*" (*Rv* 1:8).
As all things are produced through the Word eternally spoken,
so all things are restored, advanced and completed through
the Word united to flesh. Therefore he is truly and properly
called Jesus, *because there is no other name under heaven
given to men by which one can obtain salvation* (*Ac* 4:12).

St Bonaventure
The Tree of Life

Psalm

You are the fairest of the children of men
and graciousness is poured upon your lips:
because God has blessed you for evermore.

O mighty one, gird your sword upon your thigh;
in splendour and state, ride on in triumph
for the cause of truth and goodness and right.

Take aim with your bow in your dread right hand.
Your arrows are sharp: peoples fall beneath you.
The foes of the king fall down and lose heart.

Your throne, O God, shall endure for ever.
A sceptre of justice is the sceptre of your kingdom.
Your love is for justice; your hatred for evil.

Therefore God, your God, has anointed you
with the oil of gladness above other kings:
your robes are fragrant with aloes and myrrh.

From the ivory palace you are greeted with music.
The daughters of kings are among your loved ones.
On your right stands the queen in gold of Ophir.

Psalm 44 (45):3-10

Prayers

Believing, hoping, and loving
with my whole heart, with my whole mind,
    and with my whole strength,
may I be carried to you, beloved Jesus,
as to the goal of all things,
because you alone are sufficient,
you alone are good and pleasing
to those who seek you and love your name.
For you, my good Jesus,
are the redeemer of the lost,
the saviour of the redeemed,
the hope of exiles,
the strength of labourers,
the sweet solace of anguished spirits,

the crown and imperial dignity
of the triumphant,
the unique reward and joy
of all the citizens of heaven,
the renowned offspring of the supreme God
and the sublime fruit of the virginal womb,
    the abundant fountain of all graces,
of whose fullness we have all received.

St Bonaventure
The Tree of Life

Ah, most sweet Jesus, mortify within me all that is bad. Put to death in me all that is vicious and unruly. Kill whatever displeases thee. Mortify within me all that is my own. Give me true humility, true patience, and true charity. Grant me perfect control of my tongue, my senses, and all my members. Adorn me with thy merits and virtues. Prepare for thyself, for thyself only, a pleasing tabernacle, a delightful dwelling for thyself within me. Renew my spirit, my soul, and my body with thy grace. Conform me to thy sacred Manhood. Reform the faculties of my soul through the most holy faculties of thy Soul. Remake me according to thy own Heart. Give me true simplicity of soul, that I may seek only thee. Enlighten my mind. Grant me grace to unite myself to thee in my soul without let or hindrance from created things. Kindle within me the fire of thy love. Consume me in thy fire. Transform me, that nothing may live within me, but thee only, O Lord.

Ludovicus Blosius
Book of Spiritual Instruction

By what boundless mercy, my Saviour,
have you allowed me to become
a member of your body:
me, the unclean, the defiled, the prodigal? How is it that
you have clothed me
in the brilliant garment
radiant with the splendour of immortality, which turns
all my members into light?
Your body, immaculate and divine,
is all radiant with the fire of your divinity,
with which it is ineffably joined and combined. This is
the gift you have given me, my God:
that this mortal and shabby frame has become one with
your immaculate body
and that my blood has been mingled
with your blood.
I know, too, that I have been made one
with your divinity and have become
your own most pure body, a brilliant member,
transparently lucid, luminous and holy.
I see the beauty of it all.
I can gaze on the radiance.
I have become a reflection of your grace.

St Symeon the New Theologian
Hymns of Divine Love

For Faith in the Holy Spirit

Meditation

This is contemplation: the simple gaze of God upon His Word, of the Word upon His Father. From this contemplation is born mutual wonder and love of the divine nature, the love of two Persons…. It is an act of infinite Love, substantial Love, the third Person of the Blessed Trinity. The two Persons are forever united in the common breathing forth of the one Love which flows between them and fills them with joy.

He is given to us; it is He who breathes in us. He sighs toward the Infinite whence He comes. The Spirit makes us sigh for the infinite One. The filial Spirit within us aspires to the Father and aspires also, the saints tell us, to our Mother, the Virgin Mary. He wishes to raise us to this infinite One whence we came, this Father whose children we are through grace. It is the Spirit who carries us, who leads us.

This is what God is!

Marie-Eugene of the Child Jesus
Where the Spirit Breathes

Psalm

O where can I go from your spirit,
or where can I flee from your face?
If I climb the heavens, you are there.
If I lie in the grave, you are there.

If I take the wings of the dawn
and dwell at the sea's furthest end,
even there your hand would lead me,
your right hand would hold me fast.

If I say: "Let the darkness hide me
and the light around me be night,"
even darkness is not dark for you
and the night is as clear as the day.

From Psalm 138 (139)

Prayer

Come, Holy Spirit, fill the hearts of your faithful,
and enkindle in them the fire of your love.
V. Send forth your Spirit and they shall be created.
R. And you shall renew the face of the earth.

Let us pray:
O God, who has taught the hearts of the faithful by the
light of the Holy Spirit,
grant that by the gift of the same Spirit
we may be always truly wise and ever rejoice
in his consolation.
R. Amen

Veni Creator Spiritus

Come, Holy Spirit, Creator, come
from thy bright celestial throne.
Come, take possession of our souls,
and make them all thy own.

    Thou who art called the Paraclete,
    best gift of God above,
    the living spring, the living fire,
    sweet unction and true love.

Thou who art sevenfold in thy grace,
finger of God's right hand;
his promise, teaching little ones
to speak and understand.

    O guide our minds with thy blest light,
    with love our hearts inflame;
    and with thy strength which never decays,
    confirm our mortal frame.

Far from us drive our deadly foe;
true peace unto us bring;
and through all perils lead us safe
beneath thy sacred wing.

    Through thee may we the Father know,
    through thee the eternal Son,
    and thee, the Spirit of them both,
    thrice-blessed Three in One.

All glory to the Father be,
with his co-equal Son;
the same to thee, great Paraclete,
while endless ages run.

The Blessed Virgin Mary

Sub Tuum Praesidium

In the shadow of your mercy we shelter,
O Mother of God.
Do not ignore our supplications
in our temptation,
but deliver us from danger,
O pure one, blessed one.

Egyptian papyrus, 2nd century

The Memorare

Remember, O most loving Virgin Mary, that never was it known that anyone, in any age, who fled to your protection, implored your help, or sought your intercession was ever abandoned. Inspired with this confidence, we fly unto you, O virgin of virgins, our mother. To you do we come, before you we stand, sinful and sorrowful. Do not, O mother of the Word incarnate, despise our prayers, but graciously hear and grant them.

The Holy Rosary for Year of Faith

(Meditations by Bl John-Paul II)

I. The Joyful Mysteries (Mondays, Saturdays)

෯෯෯

1. The Annunciation (*Lk* 1:26-38)

   Mary uttered this *fiat in faith*. In faith she trusted herself
   to God without reserve and devoted herself totally as the
   handmaid of the Lord to the person of her Son. And this
   Son … she conceived in her mind before she conceived
   him in her womb: precisely in faith.

   Redemptoris Mater 13

2. The Visitation (*Lk* 1:39-45)

   The *fullness of grace* announced by the angel means
   the gift of God himself. *Mary's faith,* proclaimed by
   Elizabeth at the Visitation, indicates *how* the Virgin of
   Nazareth *responded to this gift*.

   Redemptoris Mater 12

3. The Nativity (*Lk* 2:1-7)

   The Nativity makes us to reflect on the central and
   determinative event of history: the Incarnation of God!
   We adore the Babe of Bethlehem, the Son of God, the
   Word by whom everything was created and without
   whom nothing was made of all that exists.

   Rome, 30.12.1981

4. The Presentation in the Temple (*Lk* 2:22-35)

Simeon's words cast new light on the announcement which Mary had heard from the angel: Jesus is the Saviour; he is "a *light* for revelation" to mankind.

Redemptoris Mater 16

5. The Finding of the Child Jesus (*Lk* 2:41-52)

Jesus was aware that "no one knows the Son except the Father" (*Mt* 11:27); thus even his Mother, to whom had been revealed most completely the mystery of his divine sonship, lived in intimacy only through faith!

Redemptoris Mater 17

II. The Luminous Mysteries (Thursdays)

෴

1. The Baptism of the Lord (*Mt* 3:13-17)

Christian spirituality is distinguished by the disciple's commitment to become conformed ever more fully to his Master (cf. *Rm* 8:29; *Ph* 3:10, 12). The outpouring of the Holy Spirit in Baptism grafts the believer like a branch onto the vine which is Christ (cf. *Jn* 15:5) and makes him a member of Christ's mystical Body (cf. *1 Co* 12:12; *Rm* 12:5).

Rosarium Virginis Mariae 15

2. The Marriage at Cana (*Jn* 2:1-12)

Mary places herself between her Son and mankind in the reality of their wants, needs and sufferings. Her mediation is thus in the nature of intercession: Mary "intercedes" for mankind. And that is not all. As a mother she also wishes the messianic power of her Son to be manifested, that salvific power of his which is meant to help man in his misfortunes, to free him from the evil which in various forms and degrees weighs heavily upon his life.

Redemptoris Mater 21

3. The Proclamation of the Kingdom and the call to conversion (*Mk* 1:14-15; 2:3-12)

To convert oneself is an expression of profound significance. It means, in the spiritual dimension, to change the direction of one's own life: to open oneself to faith, to pass from the cult of material things to the intelligent use of them as instruments for the better service of God and one's neighbour; to pass from worldly dissipation to Christian integrity, from disillusion and dejection to the hope and joy of an existence full of meaning.

Rome, 24.01.1993

4. The Transfiguration (*Lk* 9:28-36)

To look upon the face of Christ, to recognise its mystery amid the daily events and the sufferings of his human life, and then to grasp the divine splendour definitively revealed in the Risen Lord, seated in glory at the right hand of the Father: this is the task of every follower of Christ and therefore the task of each one of us.

In contemplating Christ's face we become open to receiving the mystery of Trinitarian life, experiencing ever anew the love of the Father and delighting in the joy of the Holy Spirit.

Rosarium Virginis Mariae 9

5. The Institution of the Eucharist (*Mt* 26:26-29)

A final mystery of light is the institution of the Eucharist, in which Christ offers his body and blood as food under the signs of bread and wine, and testifies "to the end" his love for humanity (*Jn* 13:1), for whose salvation he will offer himself in sacrifice.

Rosarium Virginis Mariae 21

III. The Sorrowful Mysteries (Tuesdays, Fridays)

1. The Agony in Gethsemane (*Mk* 14:32-42)

The intensity of the episode of the agony in the Garden of Olives passes before our eyes. Oppressed by foreknowledge of the trials that await him, and alone before the Father, Jesus cries out to him in his habitual and affectionate expression of trust: "Abba, Father".

Novo Millennio Ineunte 25

2. The Scourging at the Pillar (*Mt* 27:15-26)

Every man has *his own share in the Redemption*. Each one is also *called to share in that suffering* through which the Redemption was accomplished. He is called to share in that suffering through which all human suffering has also been redeemed. In bringing about the Redemption through suffering, Christ *has* also raised *human suffering to the level of the Redemption.*

Salvifici Doloris 19

3. The Crowning with Thorns (*Mt* 27:27-31)

Those who share in the sufferings of Christ preserve in their own sufferings a very special *particle of the infinite treasure* of the world's Redemption, and can share this treasure with others. The more a person is threatened by sin, the heavier the structures of sin which today's world brings with it, the greater is the eloquence which human suffering possesses in itself.

Salvifici Doloris 27

4. The Carrying of the Cross (*Lk* 23:26-32)

Following him on the way to Calvary, they learn the meaning of salvific suffering. And how could one contemplate Christ carrying the Cross and Christ Crucified, without feeling the need to act as a "Simon of Cyrene" for our brothers and sisters weighed down by grief or crushed by despair?

Rosarium Virginis Mariae 25, 40

5. The Crucifixion and Death (*Lk* 23:33-38, 44-46)

As though by a continuation of that motherhood which by the power of the Holy Spirit had given him life, the dying Christ conferred upon the ever Virgin Mary a *new kind of motherhood* - spiritual and universal - towards all human beings, so that every individual, during the pilgrimage of faith, might remain, together with her, closely united to him unto the Cross, and so that every form of suffering, given fresh life by the power of the Cross, should become no longer the weakness of man but the power of God.

Salvifici Doloris 26

IV. The Glorious Mysteries (Wednesdays, Sundays)

1. The Resurrection (*Mt* 28:1-8)

   Contemplating the Risen One, Christians *rediscover the reasons for their own faith* (cf. *1 Co* 15:14) and relive the joy not only of those to whom Christ appeared - the Apostles, Mary Magdalene and the disciples on the road to Emmaus - but also *the joy of Mary*, who must have had an equally intense experience of the new life of her glorified Son.

   Rosarium Virginis Mariae 23

2. The Ascension of Our Lord (*Ac* 1:6-11)

   By raising Jesus from the dead, God has conquered death, and in Jesus he has definitely inaugurated his kingdom. During his earthly life, Jesus was the Prophet of the kingdom; after his passion, resurrection and ascension into heaven he shares in God's power and in his dominion over the world.

Redemptoris missio 16

3. The Descent of the Holy Spirit (*Ac* 2:1-2)

The Holy Spirit is the gift that comes into man's heart together with prayer. The Holy Spirit not only enables us to pray, but guides us "from within" in prayer: he is present in our prayer and gives it a divine dimension. Prayer through the power of the Holy Spirit becomes the ever more mature expression of the new man, who by means of this prayer participates in the divine life.

Dominum Vivificantem 65

4. The Assumption (*1 Th* 4:13-19)

In the Ascension, Christ was raised in glory to the right hand of the Father, while Mary herself would be raised to that same glory in the Assumption, enjoying beforehand, by a unique privilege, the destiny reserved for all the just at the resurrection of the dead.

Rosarium Virginis Mariae 23

5. The Coronation of the Blessed Virgin Mary (*Rv* 12:1; 14:1-5; *Is* 6:1-3)

Crowned in glory - as she appears in the last glorious mystery - Mary shines forth as Queen of the Angels and Saints, the anticipation and the supreme realisation of the eschatological state of the Church.

Rosarium Virginis Mariae 23

The Hail, Holy Queen (Salve, Regina)

Hail, holy Queen,
Mother of Mercy,
hail our life,
our sweetness,
and our hope.
To thee do we cry,
poor banished children of Eve;
to thee do we send up our sighs,
mourning and weeping
in this vale of tears.
Turn then, most gracious advocate,
thine eyes of mercy towards us;
and after this our exile,
show unto us
the blessed fruit of thy womb, Jesus.
O clement, O loving, O sweet Virgin Mary.

V. Pray for us O holy mother of God.
R. That we may be made worthy of the promises of Christ.

Prayer

Calm,
O maiden most pure,
the wild storm of my soul,
for you alone showed yourself on earth
to be the port
of all who set a course
through the perils of life.
You who gave birth
to the Light,
brighten, O Pure Lady,
the eyes of my heart.
You were given to us on earth
as protection, bulwark and boast.
You were given to us as a tower
and sure salvation,
O maiden.
For this we no longer fear adversity,
we who devoutly glorify you.

Joseph the Studite

The Communion of Saints

St Joseph (Novena)

O glorious St Joseph, thou who hast power to render possible, things that are for us impossible, come to our aid in this present trouble and distress. *(Here mention your request)* Take this important and difficult affair under thy particular protection that it may end happily.

O dear St Joseph, all our confidence is in thee. Let it not be said that we would invoke thee in vain and since thou art so powerful with Jesus and Mary, show that thy goodness equals thy power. Amen.

Sts Peter and Paul

O God, who on the Solemnity of the Apostles Peter and Paul give us the noble and holy joy of this day, grant, we pray, that your Church may in all things follow the teaching of those through whom she received the beginnings of right religion. Through our Lord Jesus Christ, your Son, who lives and reigns with you in the unity of the Holy Spirit, one God, for ever and ever.

Collect for the Feast day

Our Patron Saint

O my heavenly Patron, St *N.*, who has vouchsafed to help me by your example and prayers, grant that I may both follow in your steps and enter your fellowship; through Jesus Christ our Lord. Amen

Catholic Prayers, 1907

The Angels (Psalm 150)

Antiphon: Bless the Lord, O angels,
you mighty ones who do God's bidding.

Alleluia!

Praise God in his holy place,
praise him in his mighty heavens.
Praise him for his powerful deeds,
praise his surpassing greatness.

O praise him with sound of trumpet,
praise him with lute and harp.
Praise him with timbrel and dance,
praise him with strings and pipes.

O praise him with resounding cymbals,
praise him with clashing of cymbals.
Let everything that lives and that breathes
give praise to the Lord. Alleluia!

Antiphon: Bless the Lord, O angels,
you mighty ones who do God's bidding.

Our Guardian Angel

O most holy angel of God, appointed by God to be my guardian, I give you thanks for all the benefits which you have ever bestowed on me in body and in soul. I praise and glorify you that you condescended to assist me with such patient fidelity, and to defend me against all the assaults of my enemies. Blessed be the hour in which you were assigned me for my guardian, my defender and my patron. In acknowledgement and return for all your loving ministries to me, I offer you the infinitely precious and noble heart of Jesus, and firmly purpose to obey you henceforward, and most faithfully to serve my God. Amen.

St Gertrude of Helfta

The Church and the World

For the Pope

O almighty and eternal God, have mercy on your servant, Pope *N*., and direct him by your mercy into the way of everlasting salvation. May he desire by your grace those things that are agreeable to you, and perform them with all his strength. Through Christ our Lord. Amen.

For Priests and Religious

Father, you have appointed your Son Jesus Christ eternal high priest. Guide those he has chosen to be ministers of word and sacrament and help them to be faithful in fulfilling they ministry they have received.

Father, you call all those who believe in you to grow perfect in love by following in the footsteps of Christ your Son. May those who have chosen to serve you as religious provide by their way of life a convincing sign of your kingdom for the Church and the whole world. Grant this through our Lord Jesus Christ, your Son, who lives and reigns with you and the Holy Spirit, one God, forever and ever. Amen.

Roman Missal

For the Deposit of Faith

I beseech the Blessed Virgin Mary, Mother of the Incarnate Word and Mother of the Church, to support with her powerful intercession the catechetical work of the entire Church on every level, at this time when she is called to a new effort of evangelisation. May the light of the true faith free humanity from the ignorance and slavery of sin in order to lead it to the only freedom worthy of the name: that of life in Jesus Christ under the guidance of the Holy Spirit, here below and in the Kingdom of Heaven, in the fullness of the blessed vision of God face to face!

Blessed John Paul II
Apostolic Constitution *Fidei Depositum*

For the Unity of Christians

Lord, hear the prayers of your people and bring the hearts of believers together in your praise and in common sorrow for their sins. Heal all divisions among Christians that we may rejoice in the perfect unity of your Church and move together as one to eternal life in your kingdom.

Roman Missal

For the Spread of the Gospel

God our Father, you will all men to be saved and come to the knowledge of the truth. Send workers into your great harvest that the gospel may be preached to every creature and your people, gathered together by the word of life and strengthened by the power of the sacraments, may advance in the way of salvation and love.

Prayer for Missions Sunday

For the Conversion of England

O Immaculate Virgin Mother of our Lord Jesus Christ, Mother of Grace, and Queen of the kingdom of thy Son, humbly kneeling before thee, we offer thee this country in which we live. It once was thine. Before it was robbed of the holy Faith all its children were thy children, and you were honoured throughout its length and breadth as its Protectress and its Queen. Again do we consecrate it to thee; again do we dedicate it as thine own Dowry. We offer our own hearts, that their love and service may ever grow and increase. We offer all our brethren - those multitudes who know thee so little or know thee not at all. May thy prayer bring back our country's ancient faith. May thy intercession lead us to a closer union with thy divine Son. We consecrate ourselves to Him through thee. Obtain for us, and for this country, thy Dowry, every grace and blessing, O clement, O loving, O sweet Virgin Mary!

V. Pray for us O Holy Mother of God:

R. That we may be worthy of the promises of Christ

Prayer for Rosary Sunday

For Peace

In peace let us pray to the Lord. R: *Lord, have mercy.*

For the peace of God and the salvation of our souls, let us pray to the Lord. R.

For peace of the whole world, for the stability of the holy churches of God, and for the unity of all, let us pray to the Lord. R.

For this holy house and for those who enter it with faith, reverence, and the fear of God, let us pray to the Lord. R.

For our Pope *N.,* our Bishop *N.,* the honourable priests, the deacons in the service of Christ, and all the clergy and laity, let us pray to the Lord. R.

For our country, her leaders, and all those in public service, let us pray to the Lord. R.

For this parish and city, for every city and country, and for the faithful who live in them, let us pray to the Lord. R.

For favourable weather, an abundance of the fruits of the earth, and temperate seasons, let us pray to the Lord. R.

For travellers by land, sea, and air, for the sick, the suffering, the captives, and for their salvation, let us pray to the Lord. R.

For our deliverance from all affliction, wrath, danger, and distress, let us pray to the Lord. R.

Help us, save us, have mercy upon us, and protect us, O God, by your grace. R.

Remembering our most holy, pure, blessed, and glorious Lady, the Theotokos and ever-virgin Mary, with all the saints, let us commit ourselves and one another and our whole life to Christ our Lord, our God, whose power is beyond compare, and glory is beyond understanding; whose mercy is boundless, and love for us is ineffable; look upon us and upon this holy house in your compassion. Grant to us and to those who pray with us your abundant mercy. R: *To you, O Lord.*

For to you belong all glory, honour, and worship to the Father and the Son and the Holy Spirit, now and forever and to the ages of ages. R: *Amen.*

Divine Liturgy of St John Chrysostom

For Religious Freedom

Christ our King, who has called us to be a light to the world and to proclaim the Gospel to all peoples, we ask for the preservation of religious freedom in our land. Grant unto us, by the merits of your passion and death: lucidity of mind, strength of spirit, and purity of heart, so that we may readily defend our religious liberty wherever it is under threat; that we may be able to keep the faith of your Holy Church; and that we may affirm truth in the face of error, display virtue in the presence of evil, and retain unity in a time of discord.

O Lord, we are made in your image and likeness. Guard, we beseech you, the freedom and integrity of conscience of all called to faith in you, that they may in truth love and serve you forever. For it is in your Holy Name we pray. Amen.

Editor

For Marriage

Heavenly Father,

Through the powerful intercession of the Holy Family, grant to this local Church the many graces we need to foster, strengthen, and support faith-filled, holy marriages and holy families.

May the vocation of married life, a true calling to share in your own divine and creative life, be recognised by all believers as a source of blessing and joy, and a revelation of your own divine goodness.

Grant to us all the gift of courage to proclaim and defend your plan for marriage, which is the union of one man and one woman in a lifelong, exclusive relationship of loving trust, compassion, and generosity, open to the conception of children.

We make our prayer through Jesus Christ, who is Lord forever and ever. Amen.

Archbishop John Nienstedt

For the Sanctity of Life

Heavenly Father, through whom and for whom all things were created, we pray that your gift of human life will be protected from the instant of its natural conception until by your holy will you require that it return to you. May those who have a duty to care for life realise that it is you who cherish and sustain each unique individual human being at every moment of its existence.

Father of Christ, you sanctified life in the womb of the Blessed Virgin. You sent your only-begotten Son that all might merit to receive everlasting life. Teach us so to reverence all human life that we will dutifully safeguard and nurture each precious person until we are called to be with you forever. This we ask through Christ Jesus, Our Lord and Saviour: to him be the glory. Amen.

Editor

For the Sick

Father, your Son accepted our sufferings to teach us the virtue of patience in human illness. Hear the prayers we offer for our sick brothers and sisters. May all who suffer pain, illness or disease realise that they are chosen to be saints, and know that they are joined to Christ in his suffering for the salvation of the world, who lives and reigns with you and the Holy Spirit, one God, forever and ever. Amen.

Roman Missal

For the Faithful Departed

Out of the depths I cry to you, O Lord,
Lord, hear my voice!
O let your ears be attentive
to the voice of my pleading.

If you, O Lord, should mark our guilt,
Lord, who would survive?

But with you is found forgiveness:
for this we revere you.

My soul is waiting for the Lord,
I count on his word.
My soul is longing for the Lord
more than watchmen for daybreak.
(Let the watchman count on daybreak
and Israel on the Lord.)

Because with the Lord there is mercy
and fullness of redemption,
Israel indeed he will redeem
from all its iniquity.

Psalm 129 (130)

Personal Petitions

For Faith

O my God, thou dost over-abound in mercy! To live by faith is my necessity. Thou hast pronounced a blessing on it. Thou hast said that I am more blessed if I believe in thee, than if I saw thee. Give me to share that blessedness, give it to me in its fullness. Enable me to believe as if I saw; let me have thee always before me as if thou wert always bodily and sensibly present. Let me ever hold communion with thee, my hidden, but living God.

Bl John Henry Newman

For Hope

O my God, nothing is hard or impossible to you, because your power is infinite; and there is nothing that you are unwilling to do for us, for your mercy and goodness also are infinite. You have made us in your own image and likeness and you love the work of your hands. You have redeemed us by the precious blood of your only Son, in whom we are promised everlasting life. You have bestowed upon us your Spirit of Truth, your Holy Catholic Church, and the communion of Saints. In you, O Lord, are placed my hope and my sure foundation, and I shall never be confounded.

From *Catholic Prayers, 1907*

For Charity

O my God, with deepest faith I adore thee, bless thee, and worship thee, the one true God. I love thee and long to love thee with all my heart, all my mind, and all my strength. The angels and spirits who love thee, love me too. And I love them in thee. Therefore, let us adore thee, God the Father, who created us and gave us life. Let us worship thee, Wisdom of the father who renewed his likeness in us. Let us bless thee, Holy Spirit, for we love in thee and through thee. Let us praise thee, Most Holy Trinity, Three Persons in One God, who makest us to live through thee and in thee. To thy likeness we are made: reshape us in thy image. May we love thee in all creatures and all creatures in thee. Amen.

William of St Thierry

For Humility

Lord Jesus Christ, grant that I may be free from unholy desires, and that, for your love, I may remain obscure and unknown in this world, to be known only to you. Do not permit me to attribute to myself the good that you perform in me and through me, but rather, referring all honour to you, may I admit only to my infirmities, so that renouncing sincerely all vainglory which comes from the world, I may aspire to that true and lasting glory that comes from you. Amen

St Frances Xavier Cabrini

For Wisdom

Oh light of the world, infinite God, Father of eternity, giver of wisdom and knowledge, and ineffable dispenser of every spiritual grace; who knowest all things before they are made, who makest the darkness and the light; put forth thy hand and touch my mouth, and make it as a sharp sword to utter eloquently thy words. Make my tongue, O Lord, as a chosen arrow, to declare faithfully thy wonders. Put thy Spirit, O Lord, in my heart that I may perceive; in my soul, that I may retain; and in my conscience that I may meditate. Do thou lovingly, holily, mercifully, clemently and gently inspire me with thy grace. Do thou teach, guide and strengthen the comings in and goings out of my senses and my thoughts. And let thy discipline instruct me even to the end, and the counsel of the Most High help me through thy infinite wisdom and mercy. Amen.

St Anthony of Padua

For Patience

Lord, let nothing disturb me,
nothing affright me,
All things are passing;
thou never changeth.
Patient endurance
attaineth to all things.
Who possesseth thee
in nothing is wanting:
thou alone, Lord, sufficeth.

St Teresa of Avila

For Final Perseverance

Stay with me, Lord, for it is necessary to have you present so that I do not forget you. You know how easily I abandon you.

Stay with me, Lord, because I am weak and I need your strength, that I may not fall so often.

Stay with me, Lord, for you are my life, and without you, I am without fervour.

Stay with me, Lord, for you are my light, and without you, I am in darkness.

Stay with me, Lord, to show me your will.

Stay with me, Lord, so that I hear your voice and follow you.

Stay with me, Lord, for I desire to love you very much, and always be in your company.

Stay with me, Lord, if you wish me to be faithful to you.

Stay with me, Lord, for as poor as my soul is, I wish it to be a place of consolation for you, a nest of love.

Stay with me, Jesus, for it is getting late and the day is coming to a close, and life passes, death, judgement, eternity approaches. It is necessary to renew my strength, so that I will not stop along the way and for that, I need you. It is getting late and death approaches. I fear the darkness, the temptations, the dryness, the cross, the sorrows. O how I need you, my Jesus, in this night of exile!

Stay with me tonight, Jesus, in life with all its dangers, I need you.

Let me recognise you as your disciples did at the breaking of bread, so that the Eucharistic Communion be the light which disperses the darkness, the force which sustains me, the unique joy of my heart.

Stay with me, Lord, because at the hour of my death, I want to remain united to you, if not by Communion, at least by grace and love.

Stay with me, Jesus, I do not ask for divine consolation, because I do not merit it, but, the gift of your presence, oh yes, I ask this of you!

Stay with me, Lord, for it is you alone I look for: your love, your grace, your will, your heart, your Spirit, because I love you and ask no other reward but to love you more and more.

With a firm love, I will love you with all my heart while on earth and continue to love you perfectly during all eternity. Amen

St Pio of Pietrelcina

Adoration and Devotion

Before the Blessed Sacrament

Would that I might obtain this favour, Lord, to find thee alone and by thyself, to open unto thee my whole heart, and enjoy thee even as my soul desireth; and that henceforth none may look upon me, nor any creature move me, nor have regard to me; but that thou alone mayest speak unto me, and I to thee, as the beloved is wont to speak to his beloved, and friend to feast with friend.

Ah, Lord God, when shall I be wholly united to thee, and absorbed by thee, and become altogether forgetful of myself? "Thou in me, and I in thee;" so also grant that we may both continue together in one.

O unspeakable grace! O admirable condescension! O immeasurable love specially bestowed on one such as me. What return shall I make to thee, O Lord, for this grace, for charity so unparalleled? There is nothing else that I am able to present more acceptable than to offer my heart wholly to thee, my God. Vouchsafe, O Lord, to remain with me, and I gladly with thee.

Thomas à Kempis

The Divine Praises

Blessed be God.

Blessed be his Holy Name.

Blessed be Jesus Christ, true God and true man.

Blessed be the name of Jesus.

Blessed be his Most Sacred Heart.

Blessed be Jesus in the Most Holy Sacrament of the altar.

Blessed be the Holy Spirit, the Paraclete.

Blessed be the great Mother of God, Mary most holy.

Blessed be her holy and Immaculate Conception.

Blessed be her glorious Assumption.

Blessed be the name of Mary, Virgin and Mother.

Blessed be St Joseph, her spouse most chaste.

Blessed be God in his angels and in his Saints.

May the heart of Jesus, in the Most Blessed Sacrament, be praised, adored, and loved with grateful affection, at every moment, in all the tabernacles of the world, even to the end of time. Amen.

Litany to the Holy Name of Jesus

V. Lord, have mercy on us.

R. Christ, have mercy on us.

V. Lord, have mercy on us. Jesus, hear us.

R. Jesus, graciously hear us.

V. God the Father of Heaven

R. Have mercy on us.

V. God the Son, Redeemer of the world,
R. Have mercy on us.
V. God the Holy Spirit,
R. Have mercy on us.
V. Holy Trinity, one God,
R. Have mercy on us.
V. Jesus, Son of the living God,
R. Have mercy on us. (Repeat)
Jesus, splendour of the Father,
Jesus, brightness of eternal light,
Jesus, King of glory,
Jesus, sun of justice,
Jesus, Son of the Virgin Mary,
Jesus, most amiable,
Jesus, most admirable,
Jesus, the mighty God,
Jesus, Father of the world to come,
Jesus, angel of great counsel,
Jesus, most powerful,
Jesus, most patient,
Jesus, most obedient,
Jesus, meek and humble of heart,
Jesus, lover of chastity,
Jesus, lover of us,
Jesus, God of peace,
Jesus, author of life,

Jesus, example of virtues,
Jesus, zealous lover of souls,
Jesus, our God,
Jesus, our refuge,
Jesus, father of the poor,
Jesus, treasure of the faithful,
Jesus, good Shepherd,
Jesus, true light,
Jesus, eternal wisdom,
Jesus, infinite goodness,
Jesus, our way and our life,
Jesus, joy of Angels,
Jesus, King of the Patriarchs,
Jesus, Master of the Apostles,
Jesus, teacher of the Evangelists,
Jesus, strength of Martyrs,
Jesus, light of Confessors,
Jesus, purity of Virgins,
Jesus, crown of Saints,

V. Be merciful, R. *spare us, O Jesus.*
V. Be merciful, R. *graciously hear us, O Jesus.*

V. From all evil, R. *deliver us, O Jesus.*
From all sin, R. *deliver us, O Jesus. (Repeat)*
From your wrath,
From the snares of the devil,
From the spirit of fornication,

From everlasting death,
From the neglect of your inspirations,
By the mystery of your holy incarnation,
By your nativity,
By your infancy,
By your most divine Life,
By your labours,
By your agony and passion,
By your cross and dereliction,
By your sufferings,
By your death and burial,
By your resurrection,
By your ascension,
By your institution of the Most Holy Eucharist,
By your joys,
By your glory,

V. Lamb of God, who takest away the sins of the world,
R. spare us, O Jesus.
V. Lamb of God, who takest away the sins of the world,
R. graciously hear us, O Jesus.
V. Lamb of God, who takest away the sins of the world,
R. have mercy on us, O Jesus.
V. Jesus, hear us.
R. Jesus, graciously hear us.

Let us pray.

O Lord Jesus Christ, who never fail to help and govern those whom you bring up in your steadfast love; keep us, we beseech thee, under the protection of thy providence, and make us have a perpetual fear and love for thy Holy Name; who lives and reigns with the Father and the Holy Spirit, one God, world without end. *R. Amen.*

Prayer

I love you, O my God, and my only desire is to love you until the last breath of my life. I love you, O my infinitely lovable God, and I would rather die loving you, than live without loving you. I love you, Lord, and the only grace I ask is to love you eternally. My God, if my tongue cannot say in every moment that I love you, I want my heart to repeat it to you as often as I draw breath.

St Jean-Marie Vianney

A Novena in Thanks for Faith

O give thanks to the Lord, for he is good;
His steadfast love endures forever!

Hymn

Now thank we all our God
With heart and hands and voices,
Who wondrous things hath done,
In whom this world rejoices;
Who from our mother's arms
Hath blessed us on our way
With countless gifts of love,
And still is ours today.

O may this bounteous God
Through all our life be near us,
With ever-joyful hearts
And blessed peace to cheer us,
And keep us in his grace,
And guide us when perplexed,
And free us from all ills
In this world and the next.

All praise and thanks to God
The Father now be given,
The Son, and him who reigns
With them in highest heaven,

The one eternal God,
Whom earth and heaven adore;
For thus it was, is now,
And shall be evermore.

Martin Rinkart, tr. Catherine Winkworth

Psalm 115 (116):12-19

Antiphon: I will offer to you the sacrifice of thanksgiving
and call on the name of the Lord.

How can I repay the Lord
for his goodness to me?
The cup of salvation I will raise;
I will call on the Lord's name.

My vows to the Lord I will fulfil
before all his people.
O precious in the eyes of the Lord
is the death of his faithful.

Your servant, Lord, your servant am I;
you have loosened my bonds.
A thanksgiving sacrifice I make:
I will call on the Lord's name.

My vows to the Lord I will fulfil
before all his people,
in the courts of the house of the Lord,
in your midst, O Jerusalem.

Antiphon: I will offer to you the sacrifice of thanksgiving
and call on the name of the Lord.

Psalm Prayer

Almighty God, Father of all mercies, we give you humble and heartfelt thanks for all thy goodness and loving-kindness. By your Holy Spirit we pray that we may always offer you the sacrifice of praise, through Jesus Christ our blessed Lord and Saviour. Amen.

Reading: Lk 10:21-24

It was then that, filled with joy by the Holy Spirit, he said, 'I bless you, Father, Lord of heaven and of earth, for hiding these things from the learned and the clever and revealing them to mere children. Yes, Father, for that is what it pleased you to do. Everything has been entrusted to me by my Father; and no one knows who the Son is except the Father, and who the Father is except the Son and those to whom the Son chooses to reveal him.'

Then turning to his disciples he spoke to them in private, 'Happy the eyes that see what you see, for I tell you that many prophets and kings wanted to see what you see, and never saw it; to hear what you hear, and never heard it'.

Response

With you is the fountain of life, O Lord.
R: In your light we see light.

Meditation

If I have already told you all things in my Word, my Son,
and if I have no other word, what answer or revelation
can I now make that would surpass this? Fasten your eyes
on him alone because in him I have spoken and revealed
all and in him you will discover even more than you ask
for and desire…For as the Apostle says: "in Christ all the
fullness of the divinity dwells bodily" (*Col* 2:9).

St John of the Cross

Canticle: Rv 15:3-4

How great and wonderful are all your works,
Lord God Almighty;
just and true are all your ways,
King of nations.
Who would not revere and praise your name, O Lord?
You alone are holy,
and all the pagans will come and adore you
for the many acts of justice you have shown

Litany of Faith

Lord, have mercy upon me.
Christ, have mercy upon me.
Lord, have mercy upon me.

O God the Father of heaven, R. *Have mercy on me.*
O God the Son, Redeemer of the world, R.
O God the Holy Spirit, R.
O Holy Trinity, one God, R.

62

Thou, who being eternal truth,
canst not deceive, R.

Thou, who being infallible wisdom
canst not be deceived, R.

Thou, who hast built thy Church
on an immovable rock, R.

Thou, who hast promised
continual succour to thy Church, R.

That thou art the one true God, who
rewards the good and punishes evil,
R. *I believe firmly, O my God.*

That thou art one in essence and three in Person, R.

That thy divine Son became man
and died for the salvation of the world, R.

All that thou hast revealed in Holy Scripture; all that Jesus
Christ has taught us in his Holy Gospel; all that the holy
Apostles have preached; all that the General Councils have
declared truths of faith; all that the Catholic Church orders
me to believe, R.

All articles of faith, written and unwritten, R.

Without any hesitation or doubt; with an entire submission
of my mind; with a perfect consent of my will; with an
interior and exterior confession, R.

On account of Thy supreme majesty; on account of Thy
infallible word; on account of thy veracity, and infallibility, R.

Even if it becomes for me a cause of persecution; even if I must lose all I possess; even if it costs me my life, R.

In union with the lively faith of all the just; in union with the constant faith of all the martyrs; in union with the most perfect faith of the Blessed Virgin Mary, R.

Pope Pius VI

Our Father; Hail Mary; Glory be

Closing Prayer

O my God, light of my soul, I humbly thank thee for the gift of faith; for all good things come from thee. Thou hast shown thyself to me in thy Son, thy Word to me. Thy Holy Spirit has drawn me to him, and so to thee. And thou feedest me with manna from heaven! O thou my God, what do I have that is not from thee? All is thine. All is holy. By thy will I act, in thy light I comprehend, with thy Spirit I am sanctified, and in thy immensity I am safely kept. O Blessed One! I worship thee.

Editor

Benediction

Blessing and glory and wisdom
and thanksgiving and honour
and power and might
be unto our God forever and ever! Amen

Endnotes

1 *Jm* 1:17. Cf. also *Jn* 6:44, 65.
2 *Ep* 2:8-9; *Lm* 5:21.
3 St Bonaventure, *Itinerarium mentis in Deum*, 5.1.
4 *Mt* 16: 17.
5 10:26; 11:1 ff.
6 Adolphe Tanqueray, *The Spiritual Life*, 1170.
7 *Rm* 1:19-20.
8 *Col* 1:15-18; *Heb* 1:3.
9 *Jm* 2:17, 20, 26.
10 *Heb* 11:6.
11 *Jn* 17: 22-23.
12 Barry R Pearlman, *A Certain Faith*, p. 226.
13 *Heb* 10:19-23.
14 *Rm* 8:38-39.
15 Cf. *Ac* 14:27.
16 *Ep* 3:15-19.

Acknowledgements

Page 23 Marie-Eugene of the Child Jesus (1894-1967), *Where the Spirit Breathes*, St Paul Publications, Alba House, N.Y., 1998 used with kind permission. Page 44 used with the gracious permission of Archbishop John Nienstedt of the Archdiocese of Saint Paul and Minneapolis.

Page 22 St Symeon the New Theologian, *Hymns of Divine Love*, every effort has been made by the publishers to trace the copyrights of texts used. The publishers would be grateful for any further information pertaining to acknowledgements.